"The Appointed Time Shall Come

BUT...

Don't Despise the Process"

"Transformation is a process, and as life happens there are tons of ups and downs. It's a journey of discovery - there are moments on mountaintops and moments in deep valleys of despair" Rick Warren

Table of Contents

I. Foreword

II. The Process Defined

III. Process is God's Idea

IV. Processing Believers

V. Waiting Well...Its Significance During the Process

VI. The Reality of God's Sovereignty---Overlooked and Misunderstood

VII. FOCUS: The Way to Keep from Despising the Process

VIII. Conclusion

IX. Wisdom Nuggets to Help During the Process

X. Author's Information

"The Appointed Time Will Come....

But Don't Despise the Process"

<u>Foreword</u>

I pray that you were able to read my first book, "Wait... There is An Appointed Time." This is the sequel to that book, so buckle up as we position ourselves to continue the journey towards the promise.

Life is a journey. When one ventures out on a journey, he/she usually has a specific destination in mind. Plans are made, strategies devised, then the beginning of an arduous opportunity begins. More likely than not, you can expect detours, stops, and perhaps even delays; all of these can be components of reaching your ultimate destination!

Our lives in the Kingdom of God are journeys. The unifying factor for us all as Believers is that our ultimate destination is eternal life. This journey is tailor-made, ordained if you will, for each of us individually and the Body of Christ collectively. Our God has mapped out our lives---the good, the bad, and the ugly but necessary! This journey will include triumphs as well as failures and disappointments.

Our solace comes in knowing that all things are working together for our good and that the Holy Spirit is right there helping us make it through victoriously.

Jeremiah 29:11 says, "For I know the thoughts that I think towards you, thoughts of good and not of evil, to give you an expected end." Did you know that this scripture was written based on God's decision to lead the Israelites into captivity for 70 years? Yes, God ordained that specific journey for them. It was a necessary one so that God's people would only honor the True and Living God. The Bible even says that Jesus learned obedience through the things that He suffered.

I know most of us have been given prophetic utterances concerning our lives. Some have come to past, while some have not. Let's be honest, some of the things spoken were prophetic and others just 'pathetic.'

Nevertheless, those that came from the heart of God sometimes seem so far away and out of sync with our reality. But what I have come to tell you is that before the manifestation of that word comes forth, usually there is some pruning needed to be done! God is not going to trust us with His plan and we are all jacked up. *Ugh, that will be a no!*

I have learned and am learning the essence of **Habakkuk 2:2 – 3….though the vision tarry, wait for it; for it will surely come…it will not tarry"**.

The Bible tells us that every word of God is "yes" and "amen." It is our responsibility to 'try the Spirit by the Spirit.'

This means that we hear what is said, but then ask the Holy Spirit for confirmation, clarity, and direction. Unfortunately, waiting is not an option for a lot of Christians.

Everybody's journey is different, even if there may be striking similarities. The outcome may vary, but it will not be reached without going through the process of the journey. Our God is a Promise Maker and Keeper but attaining of the promise will require process. If He said it, He will make good on it and bring it to pass.

In my 1st book, I talked about waiting. Two of the most challenging areas in the lives of Believers are waiting and the sovereignty of God. We say God is in control, but what happens when the storms of life begin to rage? Most of the time, the initial response is to rebuke the devil instead of seeking 1st the Kingdom to get God's take on the matter. Hebrews 11:1 lists the heroes of faith; careful examination of their lives will reveal that they had to go through process to get to their promise.

We love to celebrate those heroes, but quickly distance ourselves from what they had to endure to be deemed faithful heroes.

I have heard everything from Believers: "God wouldn't allow that to happen to me; God said He would give me the desires of my heart—and that's it"; as well as "that happened in the Bible days and now I'm under grace"!

Really?! Yes, we are under grace---how else would we be able to make it? God will give us the desires of our hearts when those desires are aligned with His plan for our lives. What makes us think that God won't allow us to be processed through adversity? Look at Jesus.... I am just saying......

The premise of this book is to encourage, support, and provide fortitude during these times of process.

The mountain top is usually great---we can see clear across the horizon. But those valley experiences are the ones that cause us the most angst, when we feel like we want to give up (and some of us do).

I believe wholeheartedly that **"There is a time and season and a time to every purpose under heaven." (Ecclesiastes. 3:1)** I submit 100% assuredly that the process is not a punishment, but rather the necessary pathway or prerequisite to the promise.

Once you reach your destination through process, you will be fully able to fulfill God's promise for your life.

The Bible admonishes us to desire to be like Christ in the fellowship of His sufferings.

Christ completed Hs process...the ultimate sacrifice of His life was the only pathway for Believers to eternal life.

There is an appointed time for all things, but don't despise the process.

The Process Defined

Let's be honest. Most of us prefer the promise without enduring the process. It is during the process that we really learn the ways of God. A writer wrote "Life is the classroom God uses to build character." On that note, let's segway into the term process.

What is process? Process is a noun that is defined as a series of action steps taken to achieve a particular end. Synonyms for the word process are procedure, measure, steps, methods, mechanism or approaches. Process requires transformation. **Romans 12:2 says, "We are transformed by the renewing of our minds, proving what is God's good, acceptable, and perfect will."**

The process of transformation involves several steps:

- Getting information (research, asking questions)
- Studying (what is really being said, rehearsing in your mind)
- Obtaining revelation (illumination by the Holy Spirit)
- Receiving transformation (revelation through procedures)

The best lessons are taught and learned through process, a methodical journey.

Process is a progressive course that has an expected end. Keep in mind, becoming like Jesus is a lifelong journey!

What you carry on the inside of you is too valuable to abort because of the lack of endurance through the process. Let's look at some of the processes that we may encounter in everyday life.

Food Processing

Any method used to turn fresh foods into food products is called food processing. This may include washing, chopping, pasteurizing, freezing, fermenting packaging, and cooking. Food processing also includes adding ingredients to food to extend its shelf life. Food processing may include ultra-heat, high pressure processing or modified atmosphere. Food processing may improve as well as ensure food safety, all which lends to shelf life and food preservation. Take a moment and ask yourself, "How is my shelf life?

Am I able to stand up against intense heat, make safety adjustments...basically to endure hardness as a good soldier to be profitable for the Kingdom?

Ultimately, the process of the Believer should extend our lives towards eternity, keep us safe from harm and danger while preserving us from trouble and destruction.

Hair Processing

Processing hair is what most women know of all too well. The hair is chemically treated to change its color, texture, and even style. Once the hair has been processed, it can now be transformed into an array of styles, etc. to suit the fancy of the individual. There are specific steps that should be followed in order to get the intended results. First, you must identify what products are needed to give the results that you want.

Next, follow all instructions; 1 misstep can mean the difference between gray hair and green hair. Processing hair involves going to the roots of the hair. This is where the new growth needs to be managed. Hair products haphazardly put on one's hair is a recipe for disaster!

In order to straighten out those rough areas of our lives, He must go to the root of the problem so that it can be properly taken care of. We must follow His instructions and not deviate. This process can be hard, but the results will be incredible!

Process is God's Idea

Our Heavenly Father created process and He is the Processor. Have you ever given any thought to that immutable fact; God created process.

Things just didn't come about all willy-nilly. God was intentional, methodical, and strategic in all of His processes. Let's take a look at **Genesis 1:1-31:**

1" In the beginning God created the heaven and the earth.

² And the earth was without form, and void; and darkness was upon the face of the deep. And the Spirit of God moved upon the face of the waters.

³ And God said, "Let there be light": and there was light.

⁴ And God saw the light, that it was good: and God divided the light from the darkness.

⁵ And God called the light Day, and the darkness he called Night. And the evening and the morning were the first day.

⁶ And God said," Let there be a firmament in the midst of the waters, and let it divide the waters from the waters."

[7] And God made the firmament and divided the waters which were under the firmament from the waters which were above the firmament: and it was so.

[8] And God called the firmament Heaven. And the evening and the morning were the second day.

[9] And God said, "Let the waters under the heaven be gathered together unto one place, and let the dry land appear": and it was so.

[10] And God called the dry land Earth; and the gathering together of the waters called he Seas: and God saw that it was good.

[11] And God said, "Let the earth bring forth grass, the herb yielding seed, and the fruit tree yielding fruit after his kind, whose seed is in itself, upon the earth": and it was so.

[12] And the earth brought forth grass, and herb yielding seed after his kind, and the tree yielding fruit, whose seed was in itself, after his kind: and God saw that it was good.

[13] And the evening and the morning were the third day.

¹⁴ And God said, "Let there be lights in the firmament of the heaven to divide the day from the night; and let them be for signs, and for seasons, and for days, and years:

¹⁵ And let them be for lights in the firmament of the heaven to give light upon the earth": and it was so.

¹⁶ And God made two great lights; the greater light to rule the day, and the lesser light to rule the night: he made the stars also.

¹⁷ And God set them in the firmament of the heaven to give light upon the earth,

¹⁸ And to rule over the day and over the night, and to divide the light from the darkness: and God saw that it was good.

¹⁹ And the evening and the morning were the fourth day.

²⁰ And God said, "Let the waters bring forth abundantly the moving creature that hath life, and fowl that may fly above the earth in the open firmament of heaven".

²¹And God created great whales, and every living creature that moveth, which the waters brought forth abundantly, after their kind, and every winged fowl after his kind: and God saw that it was good.

[22] And God blessed them, saying, "Be fruitful, and multiply, and fill the waters in the seas, and let fowl multiply in the earth".

[23] And the evening and the morning were the fifth day.

[24] And God said, "Let the earth bring forth the living creature after his kind, cattle, and creeping thing, and beast of the earth after his kind"": and it was so.

[25] And God made the beast of the earth after his kind, and cattle after their kind, and everything that creepeth upon the earth after his kind: and God saw that it was good.

[26] And God said, "Let us make man in our image, after our likeness: and let them have dominion over the fish of the sea, and over the fowl of the air, and over the cattle, and over all the earth, and over every creeping thing that creepeth upon the earth".

[27] So God created man in his own image, in the image of God created he him; male and female created he them.

[28] And God blessed them, and God said unto them, "Be fruitful, and multiply, and replenish the earth, and subdue it: and have dominion over the fish of the sea, and over the fowl of the air, and over every living thing that moveth upon the earth".

[29] And God said, "Behold, I have given you every herb bearing seed, which is upon the face of all the earth, and every tree, in which is the fruit of a tree yielding seed; to you it shall be for meat.

[30] And to every beast of the earth, and to every fowl of the air, and to everything that creepeth upon the earth, wherein there is life, I have given every green herb for meat": and it was so.

[31] And God saw everything that he had made, and, behold, it was very good. And the evening and the morning were the sixth day. "

The creation of the world was placed in God's mind as a process. God's omnipotence gave way for Him to just blink or a wave of His hand to create, yet He chose process.

In verse 1, you will notice that darkness was upon the face of the earth. Our God, who is full of light, could not co-exist with the darkness.

The Bible says that He spoke and there was light!

What a mighty God! But His creation process did not stop there, Oh no...but He named the light---Night and Day. You see, the process of God has purpose and meaning.

There is a specific reason why He does what He does and allows what He allows. We may not know all of the ins and outs or the whys, but He does, and He is deliberate.

Remember we are children of the light and darkness cannot co-exist in our lives either, so He must get rid of any darkness that tries to co-exist with His light!

As you read the scripture, during each of the 7 days, God was mindful of what the creation process for that day would entail. From the 2nd through the 4th day, God created.

But not only did He create, but He assigned a name as well as a purpose to His creation during the process.

Keep in mind that a process is a series of action steps taken to achieve a particular end.

He had a particular end in mind—a peaceful habitation for mankind.

On the 5th day of the earth's creation process, God made all the creatures that move in the water; and when He was finished, He said that it was good. Take a closer look... the process had purpose. These creatures were made for water. After that creation was completed, He said it was good.

This part of the process, like all the rest, was good. When God is processing His children, He does it with a purpose in mind. What I have noticed in the creation process is that within one process, another took place.

Look at verse 26. Man was made after God's own image...process. Man was called male and female...process. They were given dominion... process. God provided for them... process. In verse 31, it states that God saw everything that He had done in the creation process and He said that it 'was very good'! My brothers and sisters, I want you to see that God is a processor of His creation.

He knows what He has already ordained for our lives. He has made provisions for us while we are being processed and He says it is working together for our good. We serve a God who loves us and wants us to be His best representation on earth.

Processing Believers

Process is simply transformation. God desires to transform us into the image of His dear Son. We when first come to Christ, we come as we are...but we cannot stay that way. There is some major work that needs to be done through process. Years ago, there was a toy called Transformers. Its theme was "Transformer...more than meets the eye". Children (and lots of adults, too) loved these toys because of their unique ability to change from one state to another. You could watch a fire engine become a robot, but only by the correct process.

By carefully reconfiguring the overall makeup of the original toy, could the new toy emerge? Yes, but it would require patience, strategy, and following instructions as well as willingness to wait and see what the end would be. Failure to follow the steps may result in you having to start all over again.

In the realm of the Spirit, many believers often despise the process. Why? So glad that you asked!! Here are a few reasons that, I, grappled with while being processed by God:

1) This can't be God.

The sovereignty of God can very much be ignored or dismissed.

Some Believers embrace salvation as a" ticket to sheer happiness and joy forevermore". They are correct to an extent.

Salvation is a wonderful lifestyle, but the Bible says," it must be worked out with fear and trembling."

Though happiness is relative to the salvation experience, it is not its foundational support. Jesus tells us in His Word that we must take up our cross and follow Him daily. Your cross and my cross may differ, however, to carry each, we must have direction and strength that only comes from God. Our cross carry is a part of our reasonable service. That is key to process. Yes, God is a loving, kind, and merciful God yet He gives us specific directives to be transformed by the renewing of our minds. The Bible is emphatic when it states that the foolish things in the world are used to confound the wise. Please be more careful when ascribing the work of God to the enemy. We don't know how our "YES" to Him will manifest nor do we know what/who He will use to 'perfect those things that concern us'.

For indeed, it is our life's circumstances that God chooses to use as tools to transform us during the time of process.

2) **This is taking way too long!**

This where many Believers run into major snags during their processes.

Ever noticed that some saints seem to have a sense of entitlement? Yes, there are many kingdom benefits, but it is God that works in us both to will and to do of HIS good pleasure.

God already knows all our stories, so He deals with us from a future perspective; we can be caught up in the here and right now.

He has already orchestrated our expected end, painting across the canvas of our lives with a palette of colors and strokes that will manifest purpose and destiny. Again, our "yes" to God may mean one thing to us and something different to God, but He knows exactly what it will take to process us towards our promise. Our process starts with zeal and fervor, but somehow along the way, flames begin to flicker. The process extends longer than we had anticipated and is harder than we would have imagined; now the process becomes problematic. Our hope may diminish, complaints become more commonplace, progress has stopped, and we wind up back at square one!

3) Our actions/inactions---what does God think?

No amount of prayer, fasting, praise/worship and or giving can manipulate God's plan. His word states 'nothing before its time...that settles it.

God does want intimacy with His children; however, this intimacy does not position us to make demands on God and to have them fulfilled. Ask yourself right now "who has known the mind of God and who has been His counsellor?" **NO ONE!!**

Stop treating God as though He is the servant. The optimum benefits from the plans that He has for us will only come when we are patient and obedient. Going ahead of God will lead to delay and frustration. If we want to share in His glory, we must embrace the fellowship of Jesus' sufferings as part of our story.

Process is painful, but oh how delightful on the other side of through!! Alignment with God---His time frames, delays, and encounters are all a part of the process. We serve a purposeful God!

Repeat this short prayer while enduring process:

"Dear Heavenly Father,

Our limited strength, imperfect wisdom, and limited abilities are just a few reasons why we need you to process us. Order our steps in your Word and transform us into the image of your dear Son. Produce in us a spirit of perseverance as we are being processed for your glory." May we remain steadfast, unmovable, always abounding in the work of the Lord in as much as we know that our labor is not in vain in the Lord."

In Jesus' name, Amen.

God wants to turn our pressure, stretching, and discomfort of the process into transforming power. Think about the process of refining gold. The refining fire is hot and steady, but after purification, a magnificent product emerges. The naked eye may not be unable to distinguish between 18 kt gold and 18 kt gold overlay, but satan can tell who has been chosen in the furnace of affliction. Going through the process distinguishes you from others and positions you for Kingdom success.

As a reminder, again, have you considered the magnitude of your "yes" to God? Our answer is usually based on the temporary; His response is based on eternity! He wants us to focus on the eternal, not the temporary. Our disposition during the process can become so negative and ungrateful that the progress that we had made stops; some may even have to recalibrate and start over. Despising what God allows is a slap in His face—as if someone else could do a better job orchestrating our lives than the CEO of the universe!!

A closer look at the processes of a few Bible characters may give you better insight into how God chooses to process His children.

The Three Hebrew Boys in the Fiery Furnace

In Daniel 3, we learn about the plight, the process, and the promise of the three Hebrew boys, Shadrach, Meshach, and Abednego.

These mighty men of valor were processed so that the glory of God could be revealed, leading to their elevation in the kingdom. The enemy used people within their sphere of influence to orchestrate and plot their demise. Yes, it may (and most likely will be) those closest to us who will be used as tools to process us! This might make the process even more painful to endure.

The three Hebrew boys were lovers of God, men of prayer, men of faith.

Because of their unwillingness to cease from praying to their God, they were sentenced to a fiery furnace process. To most, it may seem as though the fiery furnace was a harsh punishment---thrown into a fiery furnace for executing your reasonable service? What? They did not try to squirm their way out of the process. I believe that they had probably hoped for God's deliverance from this 'hot' trial, but that was not the case.

They waited for God to deliver, but He did not! But look at their perspective concerning this process: "We know that God can deliver us from this...but even if He doesn't, we are going to still praise Him!!!

No "woe is me" uttered from their lips. Their fate was sealed (or so some thought) as they entered the furnace fully clothed from head to toe. But the enemy failed to realize that God gives His own "the garment of praise for the spirit of heaviness."

Not only that, but upon investigation, there was a fourth man in the fire with them. The Son of Man showed up and delivered them. The three Hebrew boys came out of the fire unscathed, clothes not singed yet full of faith and gratitude.

They sure didn't look like the process they had endured. The process was only progression to their elevation in God—names were changed, status elevated, but most important was the fact God had a platform from which He could be magnified and draw men/women unto Himself.

Why do you think that certain things are put into the Bible?

They are not just to make us feel good, but to remind us how to behave when we endure hardness (process) as a good soldier.

The Sovereign God can allow a process that is long and hard yet oh so necessary. We may say," Couldn't He have chosen another way?" Who has known the mind of God and who has been His Counsellor?

The Sovereign God is unapologetically sovereign! He answers to Himself! He is God ALONE! If we love Him...if we trust Him...then we can rest assured that He knows what He's doing when He allows certain challenges to come into our lives.

Keep your eyes on Jesus, the author and finisher of your faith. There is always purpose in our process if we allow God to be in control. Isn't funny how we love the results of the process, but repel the process itself?

Ok ya'll...it's time to grow up so that we can go up a little higher.

Even though this may be a new experience, we serve the same God who always brings us through.

The Woman with the Issue of Blood

Sometimes our process is born as a direct result of us coming to the end of our rope. We finally decide to cry 'uncle'.

But when we get to the end or ourselves, we must tie a knot in the rope and hold on because help is on the way. So is the story of the woman with the issue of blood.

Leviticus 15 speaks of a woman's excessive blood flood as unclean. In **Luke 8:43 -48**, this woman had hemorrhaged for 12 years. The Bible says that she exhausted all of her resources on physicians. Because of her condition, this woman was separated from family and friends.

Imagine, resources are depleted, isolation, social disconnect yet she had to keep going to get relief for her body. Nothing else had worked, but she had heard about Jesus and how He had healed many. Somehow, some way, she had to get to the One she believed who could help her. Her process had to be carefully and strategically executed.

If anyone had discovered her in the midst as being unclean, it would not go well for her!

The woman with the issue of blood could not just walk up to Jesus without hesitation; her process included her having to maneuver through the throngs of people while ensuring that she was thoroughly insulated so as not to allow her condition to be readily noticed; total covering was a must, leakage was not an option.

She was on a mission. Her process may have been involved, but we understand that when the going gets tough...the tough gets going. Her process continued when she saw the massive amounts of people who, also, were seeking some type of relief from Jesus.

She had to figure how to get to Jesus while staying under the crowd's radar without discovery. But while she is trying to get to Jesus, we see in Luke another person who was being processed named Jairus.

Jairus was upfront, seeking healing for his daughter while the woman with the issue of blood was moving around undercover.

The book of Luke says that Jairus fell in front of Jesus while the woman with the issue of blood fell down behind Jesus. Both realized that He was the source that they had to be connected to in order to get relief for what ailed them. It doesn't matter about the mechanics of a process for one or another; there will be a resolution!

God is sovereign and He knows what it will take for each of us to get our desired results. The spirit of comparison can hinder your process—what God has for you is for you!

Let me reiterate! We must trust and obey. Father knows best, so stop complaining, being agitated, and complacent; those actions will not cause Him to change that which He has already mapped out for your life. Follow His instructions...plain and simple! Believers, obliterate the spirit of comparison in your lives. It causes strife and tension, and it saddens God's heart.

God knows how to complete a work in us. He will manifest His glory on earth, and He alone decides which process will be most effective and beneficial to His kingdom. Embrace the sovereignty of God and I guarantee processing will be easier.

Your process may look similar to someone else's; however, the common factor is found in **Jeremiah 29:11,** "the expected end."

For some, your process may take 20 minutes, while another may take 20 years; regardless of the length of time for manifestation of God's purpose, the benefits will outweigh the challenge of process.

No matter what type of process you must endure nor the duration, God must be glorified so that His people can be edified. The woman with the issue of blood was not only healed of her infirmity but made whole because of her faith in the Sovereign Healer.

Even though Jairus had to wait on Jesus, his daughter was still raised from the dead. Delay was not denial...what awesome expected ends they both experienced even though they had to be processed!

God's sovereignty is to be embraced as part of who we are in Him. The sooner we make the adjustments in our thinking, the processing path becomes lighter and the execution becomes more doable.

Because of who He is...we are...so why not be led by His Spirit as we are being transformed into the image of His dear Son. He loved us so much that He came down from His throne in heaven to see about us in the person of Jesus Christ.

The Sovereign God of the universe wants nothing but the BEST for those He calls His own---even during process!

Here is a prayer that I discovered to help me to embrace God's sovereignty:

"Give me, O Lord, a steadfast heart, which no unworthy affection may drag downwards; Your Sovereignty, O God gives me an unconquered heart, which no tribulation can wear out; gives me an upright heart, which no unworthy purpose may tempt aside. Bestow upon me, also, O Lord our God, understanding to know you— Your acts and ways.

Give me diligence to seek You, wisdom to find You, and a faithfulness that I may finally embrace you as the One, True, and Sovereign God."

In Jesus' Name, Amen

We will delve a little deeper into the sovereignty of God a little later.

Waiting Well: Its Significance During the Process

Becoming like Jesus... being transformed into the image of God's dear Son. It all sounds so whimsical and spiritually fulfilling, yet many Believers don't realize that this change is a process. I have found that many times Believers tend to focus on a life of salvation devoid of challenges. If we really truly want to please our Heavenly Father, then our minds have to be renewed and our thoughts aligned with God's word. Ask yourself..."do I want to please God?" Our answer must be yes, Lord, yes and our goal is to know and execute His plan, ways, and purposes for our lives.

One of the components of being processed is waiting...well! Oh, some may wait for a little while and then start complaining; others may wait longer as a badge of honor, believing that God is going to give them some special recognition for their stance. Let me ask you this question. Why do you think the Bible says, **"Wait on the Lord and be of good courage and He will strengthen your heart; wait I say on the Lord. (Psalm 27:14)** It's in the Holy book not only for knowledge's sake, but for application purposes. Waiting well is progressive and a major, intrinsic part of the process.

But it must be done in faith. Scripture tells us to **"Have faith in God" (Mark 11:22).**

Whatever your circumstances may be, it can sometimes be difficult to embrace the assurance that things are going to work out. Does that mean that you don't have faith?

Absolutely not! It means that at a particular moment in time, life's challenges may seem overwhelming and out of control. Remember Jesus in the Garden of Gethsemane. His faith did not fail; He merely responded to the realization of what was before Him. He knew God's will and ultimate plan and His love for the Father catapulted Him to respond, "Nevertheless, not my will but your will be done!" In all of His agony He waited well for the promise of being resurrected on the 3rd day and having an eternal seat in glory.

Jesus is making intercession on our behalf, just as He did for Peter, so that we don't have to experience those faith failure moments. If those moments do come (and most likely they will), when the cares of this world may sidetrack our process journey, do not worry and please don't fret. Reboot, refocus, and remind yourself that you already have the victory through Christ Jesus our Lord!

Ever heard of the old saying, "Everybody wants to go to heaven, but nobody wants to die?" Guess what?!

Everybody wants God's promises, but nobody wants to be processed.

Waiting well is the part of the process that requires intended execution on the part of the Believer. We are covenant partners with the Father.

Being in covenant with someone requires both parties to do their part in the covenant relationship. God never slumbers or sleeps and He is ALWAYS faithful in doing His part. It is up to us, as Believers, to do ours.

Waiting well builds character. Oh, it's easy to be happy and upbeat when you can see all of the pieces of the promise falling into place. But what happens when nothing looks anywhere close to what God said? Again, the Word admonishes us to wait and be of good courage. Waiting well is a courageous act. It requires a healthy and stable relationship with God. You have to know, without a doubt, that He has your back.

Honestly, waiting can be painful. When our hopes and dreams have been deferred, that is not pleasurable. My precious reader, let me speak to the pain of waiting for unfulfilled dreams. It can be frustrating, but this frustration can only be soothed by learning to wait well. Stop getting stuck, waiting for fulfillment. Keep going on with your life's journey.

Do not make what you are waiting for an idol, for this will only hinder and possibly derail manifestation!

Let me say this again..."be of good courage." Don't take it personally...

God is not out to stop you from having a good life; on the contrary, He desires that you have a life of abundance. **Lamentations 3:25 says, "The Lord is good to those that wait on Him, to the person that seeks Him."**

Our peace and solace comes from staying in fellowship with God. Meaningful fellowship includes the following: praying, fasting, praising, worship, sacrifice, giving, etc. It is imperative that we hear God's voice and obey right away. The right action must be executed at the right time.

Plowing, sowing, and reaping are all a part of the harvesting process, but never do they take place at the same time.

Waiting well requires us to look out for traps and pitfalls of the enemy. Even though we may be waiting, our attitude, disposition, etc. lend to our period of waiting well. We are not going to be able to manipulate God with our behavior just because the process may be long and it appears that our fortitude to hold on is wearing down.

Here are some tidbits that you may want to **exclude** from your acts of meaningful fellowship while waiting well:

1) Running from/avoiding difficulties and challenges

Just because the process is long, please wait on God. The 4th man in the fire will never leave or forsake you.

Stop trying to manipulate people, places, and things; if what manifests is not born out of God's spirit, it will not be able to stand up under the weight of God's purpose for your life.

Listen my brothers and sisters who are believing God for a mate...wait on God. Late bloomers are just that—there is a time and a season for every purpose under heaven.

What God has for you is for you at His appointed time! God knitted you in your mother's womb, so He is fully aware of your 'biological clock'; biological clocks have nothing on our God...just ask Abraham and Sarah.

2) Complaining, murmuring, fretting, and comparing
Stay focused. In the army of the Lord, you must stay focused. Your enemy is roaming about seeking whom he may devour. He is looking for a kink in your armor so that he can wiggle his way in to distract and destroy. Sober up from a worldly mindset. Immature thinking and juvenile mindsets only position you for earthly disaster.

Discern the season and reason for your life. Will God bless you really good? Most definitely! Will God allow us to fail at some of life's challenges? Absolutely! Are both to His honor and glory? Without a doubt! Stop talking yourself out of your blessing and go through the process.
You will surely come out on the other side a better Believer in Him.

3) Playing the blame game

Whose fault is it anyway? No one is at fault. Life happens. Waiting well is a part of the Believer's benefits package. God ordains waiting well to defeat the enemy. When things seem unbearable...seek 1st the Kingdom; things seem unwarranted and so unfair...seek 1st the kingdom. It's no one's fault. We can't expect God to create, ordain, manifest, and then bless the promise. Process leads us to the promise and helps to sustain us when we receive it.

Have you noticed that when challenges come, we usually ascribe them to the enemy? Did you know that God allows them, also? Not to destroy us, but to transform us. Stop the blame...stay in the game....be determined to win at all costs.

Let me introduce you to a term God ministered to me during this pandemic. It is called 'faith fatigue'.

I know us good Christian folks don't want to believe that faith fatigue is possible. What is faith fatigue? So glad that you asked. Faith fatigue is a temporary or momentary weakness or brief faltering of our faith.

Most believers have experienced it just on the mere scripture of **Hebrews: 11:1, "the evidence of things not seen."**

Because we function through our senses, faith fatigue may overpower us when we have been holding on to faith for so long, matters get worse instead of better, and there seems to be no relief in sight.

At some point, whether we want to fess up or not, there may be a moment when we temporarily lose faith. Does it mean we don't have faith? Absolutely not!! In **Luke 22: 31 -34,** Jesus tells Peter that satan desires to sift him as wheat. Desire here means 'demands'; satan is demanding to separate Peter from what—his faith. Jesus told Peter that He is praying for him so that his **faith does not fail**; even Jesus realized that it was a possibility.

The same applies to us as Believers.

We are not super humans; only when God adds His super to our natural, do we become a 'supernatural" entity to be reckoned with. Jesus is seated at God's right hand praying for us---that our faith fails not. The Bible says His strength is made perfect in our weakness.

Whether we falter in faith or not, He holds up securely with the shield of faith (**Ephesians.6:10).**

Faith fatigue is only temporary; God will send us help in a time of need...a testimony or a word of grace to see us through.

As we draw nigh to Him, He draws nigh to us. No time for blaming...keep moving in the power of His might.
He will never leave us nor forsake us. **I Timothy 2:13 reminds us," If we are faithless, He remains faithful; He cannot deny Himself"**.

Learning to be content with God's timing in these testing times takes tenacity. He won't show up every time the same way...but He always shows up and shows out. Just settle into God's spiritual rhythm and watch Him work in us both to will and to do of His good pleasure. Experience His wonderful glory like never before. Waiting well is not a withholding moment; it is a beholding moment. God's delay does not mean denial.

Promises delayed are often realized through discomfort so that the recipient of the promise can only find comfort in the Promise Keeper! Impatience causes you to give birth to other things that invariably hinder your promise. Waiting well creates an atmosphere for manifestation:

- Perseverance towards victory
- Increase of our faith

- Receipt of other blessings while we wait. **Isaiah 30:18 declares," Blessed are those that wait on Him."**

Despising the process only leads to disappointment, distress, and spiritual retardation, staying stuck in the same place, going nowhere fast!

God wants us to trust His divine purpose even we lack clarity in the situation. We are not our circumstances! Our Heavenly Father is an "on time God" and has constructed our processes so that on the other side of through...we may enjoy the fruits of our labor.

The Reality of God's Sovereignty—Overlooked and Misunderstood

"Who has known the mind of God and who has been His counselor?" (Romans 11:34)

I believe one of the most difficult concepts for Believers to grasp is that of the sovereignty of God. The word sovereign denotes supreme rank and power of authority. Sovereign means indisputable, and preeminent, above all others in character, importance, and excellence. It depicts greatest in degree, the utmost. Let's take a closer look at these defining words so that we can solidify this as a defining moment in our lives.

Reread those descriptors about God's character! As powerful as they are, they are still limited in encapsulating who our Most Holy Father is!!! Until we see Him face to face, these will have to do. A genuine encounter with God leaves you amazed and forever changed. Saul on the road to Damascus...Moses and the Israelites crossing the Red Sea...the woman with the issue of blood...Enoch never knowing death...just a few examples of biblical agents of change when they encountered our Sovereign God.

Because of who God is, we can't leave it to chance to navigate our way through life's journeys.

His character is above all others and His ways are indisputable; therefore, our steps must be ordered by Him.

He knows the beginning, middle, and the end. How does He know? He ordained all of our lives. He has designed our path and every step that He makes is intentional. God already knows the outcome and has everything in place so that His plan is not thwarted; it is up to us to listen and obey!

How can the clay tell the potter what to do in making His creation? The Creator of the universe, Maker of all things...the Omnipresent, Omnipotent, Omniscient Lord of all...will never and can never be upstaged, overridden, upended, or manipulated by this world system. Truth be told, many Believers fall prey to the will of the enemy because of their failure to discern, to recognize, and to embrace the sovereignty of God. Unfortunately, even in the church, many feel a sense of entitlement. For what reason? Because of taking up their crosses and following Jesus? **Ugh...that will be a NO!!!** Just call that "your reasonable service."

Jesus Christ helps us to walk in the light of His Word---that is why the Word is 'a lamp unto our feet and a light unto our path'.

During our process (es), we must cast all our cares upon the Lord---His yoke is easy and His burden is light. Our limited strength, imperfect wisdom, and inadequate abilities leave us no choice but to trust in the sovereignty of God.

During the process, God releases a spirit of perseverance that produces faithfulness, fruitfulness, as well as fearlessness.

God does not just process us when He sees that we need adjustments or alignments, but sometimes the process is so that the glory of God can be revealed through us to others in a greater way.

God's sovereignty is not merely that God has the power and right to govern everything, but that He does so always and without exception! God is sovereign in both principle and practice. He is the Supreme Authority and no power or law conceived is superior to Him. Sovereignty denotes a king who has authority over a kingdom. For instance, Queen Elizabeth is the sovereign ruler over Britain, but God is Sovereign over all! He is in complete control of the universe, yet the Bible **says, "God even created evil for His purpose" (Proverbs 16:4).**

God is not bound nor limited by the behaviors of His creations. His will is unrestricted and it is the end all to be all. **James 4:13 -16** concludes by saying that we should say **"if the Lord wills..."**

This scripture should stabilize, strengthen, and encourage our relationship with the Heavenly Father. **I Peter 3:17 tells us that it is better to suffer doing well, if that should be God's will, than for doing evil.** Process involves stretching and suffering.

And guess what? God, in His sovereignty, oversees our suffering; no suffering happens to us apart from the will of God. He knows and regulates the income (process) and the outcome (promise).

Most don't want to embrace that fact, but the truth makes you free!

Once the process becomes hard or long, our whining may delay 'all things working together for our good'. So, you may feel what's the use of planning if God may interrupt or even intercept my plans? The best advice I can share with you is to seek God first in all things and sketch out your plans with an eraser nearby! If we are not led by the Holy Spirit, then He can't lead us into all truth.

Proverbs 19:21 says, "Many are the plans of the mind of a man, but it is the purpose of the Lord that will stand." Think about---sometimes His plans don't seem to make sense, but God is a God of wisdom. Even though Believers are processed for Kingdom purpose, God remains sovereign.

Was He not sovereign, even during the unjust and horrific death of His only begotten Son?! God knows all things.

Many things are beyond our mental grasp, yet this does not hinder God's supreme rule. He rules despite our ability to comprehend and or agree to the process.

We can only see the "here and now' while He marvels through eternal lenses. He unapologetically justifies His existence and rule to no one. Look at what the word of God says about His sovereignty: **(Psalm 115:3) "God does all that He pleases;" (Job 42:2) "You can do all things; no purpose of yours can be thwarted; "(Isaiah 46:10) "My counsel shall stand and I will accomplish all of my purpose."**

Nothing in this world is coincidental. This is the world's (and some Believers') dilemma---why does God allow certain things to happen while negating the manifestation of others? Who has known the mind of God? Our process may seem unfair and even unjust, but God still remains sovereign. I have witnessed countless times when a process on my journey felt that way, but oh what joy that flooded my soul on the other side of through. I want to impress this upon your hearts because a lot of Believers see God as one-dimensional. God does allow suffering during process. The crucifixion of Christ is a prime example.

The greatest injustice known to mankind was carried out by evil men, but it was according to a sovereign plan. Because of the death, burial, and resurrection of our Lord and Savior Jesus Christ, we are alive and have the opportunity for an abundant life as well as eternity with Him. God uses every circumstance to work together for our good as well as to His glory.

God's sovereignty remains a two-edged sword; it kills the flesh during process and ultimately ushers us closer to transformation into the image of His dear Son. It reminds us that we can be made whole in the midst of adversity. When we choose to identify our processing through non-biblical lenses, we self- defeat. Wanting to control our own situations/circumstances can only lead to shipwreck. Haven't we failed enough times trying to do it our own way?

Only God knows when Jesus will return and claim us as His Bride; even Jesus doesn't know when that glorious day will come...but it is coming!

Embracing the tenets of the sovereignty of God can become a mindset to help declutter one's perspective on being processed. The sooner we embrace this undeniable truth, the sooner the process can become more palatable. The intensity of the impact of the process may lessen because we understand that God is love, He is in control, and there will be an expected end.

Taking our cues from the Word of God and not the world makes our lives so much richer.

Even though we may be hurting or experiencing some level of discomfort, we still become better while being processed. 'Let go and let God' is a true saying.

Aren't you tired of seeing those plans you have etched in stone crumble before your eyes? God wants the best for us all the time.

During the moments when we fail to acknowledge the sovereignty of God--- this is a great opportunity to retrain our brains. Scores of Believers live with 'fantasy thinking'... and a sprinkle of faith. Some believe that God has given their process a nod—to work according to their plans, therefore nullifying the sovereignty of God. Divine purpose nullifies human design all the time! How can we retrain our brains? I am glad that you asked. It is called Divine exchange.

As inhabitants of this world, our brains have been wired to respond certain ways to certain stimuli.

Ephesians 4: 23 admonishes us to "be renewed in the spirit of our mind". Christ-like thoughts generate Christ-like dispositions, attitudes, tempers, and behaviors. Failure to recognize God's sovereignty leaves us open to a fleshly lifestyle and attracts us to the diabolic schemes of the enemy.

Romans 12:12 commands us in such a way that our transformation is a continuous process from the inside out. The Divine exchange allows us to decontaminate our thoughts—change our focus from self-absorbed to Spirit-absorbed.

Just because we choose to obey God does not give us a pass when we are being processed. Obedience is a part of our reasonable service, also!

The Divine exchange takes place when our fleshly thoughts and ways are replaced by the Word of God. A heavenly God disallows His children to use worldly tactics to get heavenly blessings. Our highest regard for God's sovereignty will continually remind us that no matter what...God is in control.

When we you find yourself being attacked on all sides, **Philippians 4:8 tells us to "think on things that are honest, true, pure, just, lovely and of good report"**—a Divine exchange for the fleshly responses that may be brewing.

Don't despise the process.

God is right there working it out for your good! We should not be mad, angry or even disgruntled because of what happens to us during processing. People, places and things are merely the tools used to transform us.

God will keep us in perfect peace when we keep our mind on Him—not on our situation or circumstances.

During the times of process, stay away from people "who don't get what God is doing." Even though they have good intentions, you can easily plummet into disobedience by listening to their well-meaning advice.

One of the greatest weapons during process is silence. You may think you are in this alone, but you are not.

Keeping your mouth shut disables the enemy's abilities to thwart your plans...stop talking so much! Never do I suggest 'suffering in silence'; ask the Spirit to give you a trusted friend who can walk with you, if needed. Otherwise, you may experience unnecessary disturbances in your process and your peace!

There is a reason why the Bible says that "God is our shield and buckler." Hiding under the shadow of His wing is not cowardice, but great wisdom. Our Sovereign God is above everything. No matter what, His sovereignty trumps our perspective and finite wisdom.

Knowing that God has everything in control makes waiting for the appointed time a benefit and not a liability.

Focus: The Way to Keep from Despising the Process

We live in a fallen world. As Believers, God has given us the grace to sustain our existence. To walk in and live in that grace, we must focus. It is so easy to get caught up in this world's system. If not careful, we will begin to manage our behavior based on feelings and emotions; yes, we do have feelings and emotions, but they should not be so prevalent in our day to day lives that they take us captive and render our effectiveness sterile.

Think about how easy it is to look at an issue; automatically, most people conclude the mechanics of the situation as well as their own foresighted end to the matter. Lack of focus disarms us. We are unable to see clearly, discern correctly, and execute properly the things of God. In the natural, if your vision (focus) is off, you are working from a state of ineffectiveness; so it is in the spiritual realm. Let's take a brief look at the definitions of focus:

- A direct or concerted effort
- Converge on a certain point
- Positioned to produce a clear image
- Central point

As you can glean from the definitions, focus is targeted. It requires attention, concentration as well as consistency.

Throughout the scriptural wisdom in the Bible, there are clear examples of how focus was intricately woven into the success of a situation. As we begin to explore these examples, keep in mind that they were written that we too, in times of peril, would look at those before us whose focus made a difference in their lives.

Focus point#1: Matthew 14: 22-33

Perhaps the most readily known biblical focus point had to do with Peter walking on water. Jesus and the disciples had just finished feeding the multitude of 5,000. Jesus told the disciples to get on the ship and meet Him on the other side. Jesus was dispersing the crowd; afterwards, He went away to be by Himself in order to reboot.

While the disciples were on the ship, a fierce storm arose—blustering winds and high waves. The disciples became fearful. Remember, they had just seen Jesus do the miraculous with 2 fish and 5 loaves of bread, yet they chose to focus on the storm. Isn't that just like many of us as Believers? We witness the miracle working power of God in our lives, but when an issue arises that seems to loom large, we lose focus!

Jesus knew that opposition would come even though He told them to meet Him on the other side.

As the biblical account records in Matthew 14:22-33, Jesus sees them in distress and walks out on the water.

The disciples see Jesus on the water; instead of recognizing who He is, they say it must be a spirit. They are still afraid. Peter entreats Jesus to allow him to come on the water, trying to authenticate that it was really Him; Jesus said, "Come".

Let's pause for a moment. I can't help but see in this text that even Peter initially was afraid of the storm and then afraid of the 'spirit' on the water.

Like many of us Believers, how often do we become anxious and afraid of turbulence in our lives. We see the solution to our challenge right in front of us, but become fearful to embrace the solution? Why? Because the solution God is offering us seems "out of the box" and we become afraid to move.

Jesus told Peter to come. Peter stepped out onto the water, but lost focus of Who was in front guiding him to safety. He considered the external forces beating against him to be greater than the Eternal force that had charge over the storm. When Peter lost his focus, he began to sink.

Jesus lovingly reached down and pulled him out of the water. Jesus took him back to the ship, then commanded the storm to cease!

Brothers and sisters, Jesus may not cause the storm to cease in your life during process, but know that He is right there with you, extending His grace and mercy to support you as you go through.

Regardless how God chooses to allow you to be processed, you must follow His instructions and obey right away; obey God and leave the consequences to Him!

Focus Point#2 Isaiah 26:3

Thou wilt keep him in perfect peace, whose mind is stayed on thee: because he trusteth in thee.

I want us to examine the word 'stayed'. Stayed means steadfast, attentive or focused. It asserts that one does not waiver.

A person whose mind is stayed on Jesus totally trusts Him, keeps his eyes on Him, and believes with all of his heart that his well-being will be taken care of. Just because God's children go through challenges and struggles, it does not mean that He puts our blessings on hold or stops taking care of us; on the contrary, He never leaves us nor forsakes us.

Do you remember the story of the Israelites being in bondage for 400 years?

They were in the process of deliverance. Moses had been given the charge and they were on the move towards being free from bondage.

During their deliverance process, they began to murmur and complain---forgetting how good God had been to them in providing all that they needed.

Their deliverance process was not what they hoped or desired it to be, so it took them 40 years to make a few weeks journey. They lost their focus and their attention had shifted from deliverance to their own selfish desires.

I have experienced in my walk with Christ that those days of a "snap, crackle, and pop" resolution of issues are now few and far between. In our early walk with the Lord, He allowed things to happen quickly to authenticate His Majesty to a new Believer; now, we have got to mature! God's word tells us to "endure hardness as a good soldier."

A good soldier has been trained in such a way that he knows to be victorious, he must keep his eyes on the goal...to defeat the enemy; nothing can deter him from reaching that goal.

Focus Point#3 Philippians 3:13-14

"Brethren, I count not myself to have apprehended: but this one thing I do, forgetting those things which are behind, and reaching forth unto those things which are before, 14. I press toward the mark for the prize of the high calling of God in Christ Jesus."

Question? When you are driving, which way are you facing? The only time you should look at what's behind you is a quick, abbreviated look through the rear-view mirror to ensure safety when contemplating making a shift while driving. Brothers and sisters, on this journey called life, stop looking back at your woulda...coulda...shoulda. These memories disable you and cause you to lose focus, distracting you from purpose and destiny.

The scripture tells us to forget those things behind and reach forth to the things before...all of this requires focus. Yesterday is gone and can't be re-lived. Move forward with the goal of doing better.

Verse 14 says "I press toward the mark..." Think about pressing your clothes (maybe now pandemic press is wrinkles...I'm just saying). When pressing your clothes, you continue placing heat to the fabric until the wrinkles fall out. You focus, making sure that when you are finished, your garment is presentable to wear.

Nothing needs to interfere with you present or future endeavors; get those wrinkles out of your life and keep moving forward.

Our focus is to remain committed to what God is calling us to and not get sideswiped by the cares of this world.

The New Living Translation says it this way: "I focus on one thing, forgetting the past and looking forward to what lies ahead...I press to reach the end of the race to receive my heavenly prize."

Focus Point#4: Hebrews 12:2

"Looking unto Jesus the author and finisher of our faith; who for the joy that was set before him endured the cross, despising the shame, and is set down at the right hand of the throne of God."

Crucifixion was a terrible way to die. It was shameful and humiliating. The Bible even says, "Cursed is the man that hangs on a tree." Jesus knew that He was going to have to endure excruciating pain, let alone torment and torture before He even was hung on the cross.

Remember when He was in the Garden of Gethsemane? He asked His Heavenly Father if the cup (brutal murder) could pass Him by, yet He reconciled the fact that this was the will of His father.

He knew that this would not last forever and that very soon He would be seated in heavenly places with God.

This reminds me of childbirth. My initial experience was 23 hours of labor. The only way that I was able to get through that pain was to pray and tell myself that the pain would not last forever; soon, I would be bringing forth my bundle of joy.

Focus. The joy that was set before Christ was not the pain and suffering, but the fact He was pleasing God through His obedience.

In the midst of sadness, suffering, and pain, Jesus' focus was the fact that a temporary inconvenience could not outweigh the satisfaction of returning to His Father in all of His glory! Even unto death, Jesus was attentive to the matter at hand and suffered well for our sin and salvation. Oh, praise to the Lamb of God!!

Ask yourself---does the income of your challenges outweigh the outcome of your promise? It may seem so, but don't be fooled.

The Word of God tells us that "obedience is better than sacrifice." As Believers and Disciples of Christ, we must elevate our thinking beyond how we feel when we experience trials and tribulations. During process, we must go through with the right attitude. Despising the process will keep you in it that much longer.

Think of how proud Our Daddy is when we obey His will. When we focus on the joy set before us, pleasing our Father, then the process can yield so many wonderful benefits while we are still in it.

This focus point is essential to the overall health of one's spirit and growth and development in one's relationship with the Lord.

Focus Point#5: Mark 8:22-26

"**And he cometh to Bethsaida; and they bring a blind man unto him, and besought him to touch him.**

And he took the blind man by the hand, and led him out of the town; and when he had spit on his eyes, and put his hands upon him, he asked him if he saw ought.

And he looked up, and said, I see men as trees, walking.

After that he put his hands again upon his eyes, and made him look up: and he was restored, and saw every man clearly."

In this focus point, a blind man was brought to Jesus by his friends in a village called Bethsaida. Verse 23 says that Jesus took the man by the hand and led him out of the village.

This spoke volumes to me---the simple fact that Jesus was intentional about a 1:1 encounter with this man without distraction. Sometimes, Jesus will call us to Himself, alone time with Him, if you will, so that we can focus.

After Jesus and the man were alone, Jesus spit in His eyes, laid hands on him, and then asked him what he saw. Focus.

This seemed like an unconventional way to heal, but this is how Jesus chose to manifest His glory. Our Miracle working Savior could have merely spoken a word and immediately the man's sight could have been restored; yet this miraculous healing was progressive.

The man's response to Jesus' initial touch was that he saw men walking like trees. Obviously, this man had been previously sighted because he could identify what both men and trees looked like. Jesus chose to minister to this blind man in a caring way. He was not offended because the 1st touch did not yield complete results.

Listen, sometimes it may take another touch from God to see your manifestation, however, instantaneous or progressive, it is God who is doing the work and brings forth the miraculous! Also, the blind man did not get angry or get besides himself because his vision was not immediately flawless. Saints...please take note of this and do not despise the process.

One more touch from the Master and everything changed for this man. Initially, the blind man could have started doubting the power of Jesus, but he remained focused on the task at hand---he was going to be able to see again. This is a significant focus point for us as Believers.

We may not understand the nuts and bolts or workings of our processes, but we must focus on the fact that God does not make mistakes; He is working in us both to will and to do of His good pleasure.

We shouldn't 'pigeonhole God' into processing us the same way every time. He is sovereign and knows the intent and extent of a particular process.

If you have ever gone to get your vision checked, it can be exhausting. The doctor asks you to look into a right and left screen. He/she then manipulates the various lenses so that you can have the most clear, efficient vision as possible. Sometimes adjustments must be made to get the right focus in both the right and left eyes; once this is achieved, he prescribes glasses that will best suit your ability to see clearly. Focus is the intended goal!

I also want to highlight what happened to the blind man after the 2nd touch. He did not tell Jesus that he had partial sight nor that his vision was alright; the Bible says that the blind man saw **everything clearly**.

Jesus is faithful to perform that which is asked of Him, according to His will. Focus combined with faith will bring forth fulfillment and joy to our lives!

Focus#6 Matthew 6:33

"**But seek ye first the kingdom of God, and his righteousness; and all these things shall be added unto you**".

Our last focus point directs us to the source of all things. It commands us to seek 1st the kingdom of God. Focus. Here we are admonished to prefer the eternal over the temporal.

Why do so many Believers spend countless prayer opportunities seeking after stuff? Stop it…stop it now!

The Word of God tells us how we should be conducting our lives and where our focus should be…on the Kingdom of God. What is the Kingdom of God, anyway? **Righteous, peace, and joy in the Holy Ghost is the Kingdom of God (Romans 14:17).** We can get so caught up in what we want from Him that we lose sight on who He is, "The Messiah", the One who came to deliver us from sin.

The weight of the world can be great. To overcome this weightiness, we must focus on our future goal---to live forever with the Father. This assurance can fuel us as we navigate through this life, just passing through.

Dismissing the former and embracing the present move us towards the eternal. Men and women of God, let's keep "the main thing…the main thing… accumulation of stuff in this world just ain't it!

Focus. We must shake ourselves loose from fatigue, weariness, and the pain of the last season we were in and even the present one!

Rise above those things that have distracted you and drug you through the muck and the mire. The appointed time will come as we go from process to promise, as long as we don't despise the process. Focus---keep Jesus as your #1 priority as your soar to experience your wildest dreams at the appointed time.

<u>Conclusion</u>

God does not lie, nor does He seek to disappoint. Every aspect of God is manifested with the good of His creation in mind. When we choose to align ourselves with the Word of God, our processes can be much more beneficial and fruitful. Our endurance seems stronger and don't forget about all of the wonderful nuggets we acquire along the way.

Again, brothers and sisters, I urge you this time as I did in my 1st book, wait for the appointed time; it shall come, but don't despise the process. This statement is pivotal because when you despise the process, you are basically telling God that His ways are not the best ways. He has ordained your lives before the foundation of this world and knows His intended end for each one of us. Bishop T.D. Jakes said it something like this: "Don't let the fear of an arduous process be the pallbearers of your destiny."

Presenting ourselves as 'living sacrifices' is a part of the process; we may even look like fools for Christ.

Though the process may be long, the outcome will have even longer-lasting effects. God's word will not return to Him empty.

Ask yourself, "Do I trust my heavenly Father to work out whatever I am going through for my good? The answer should be a resounding "YES!"

Well, step aside and let the process begin, continue, and or finish; once you have gotten through that one, you will be well equipped to navigate through the next. The return on the process---the promise---will be well worth the wait.

The Appointed Time Shall Come...

But...

Don't Despise the Process!

Wisdom Nuggets to Help During the Process

- When life doesn't make sense, we can still have peace…. Rick Warren

- Life is a lively process of becoming.

  Douglas MacArthur

- **He that has done a good work in you…is faithful to complete until the day of Jesus Christ.**
  Philippians 1:6 KJV

- **God lets everything happen for a reason. It's all a learning process, and you must go from one level to another… Mike Tyson**

Author's Contact Information

I am praying for you as you allow God to process you to the promise!

Author: Francine Isabel Shuford

Email: Izzyshu@aol.com

Urbecomingsarahsdaughters@gmail.com

"Don't forget to s hare the goodness of the Lord with someone else....

THE APPOINTED TIME SHALL COME

BUT...

DON'T DESPISE THE PROCESS!